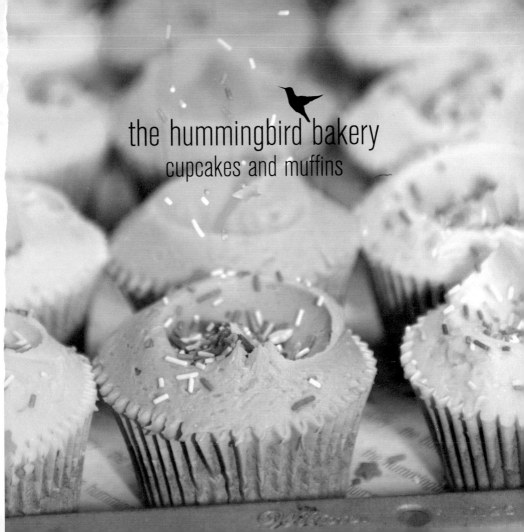

the hummingbird bakery
cupcakes and muffins

the hummingbird bakery
cupcakes and muffins

Tarek Malouf and The Hummingbird Bakers

photography by Peter Cassidy

RYLAND
PETERS
& SMALL

LONDON NEW YORK

**Design, Photographic Art Direction
and Prop Styling** Steve Painter
Senior Editor Céline Hughes
Head of Production Patricia Harrington
Art Director Leslie Harrington
Publishing Director Alison Starling

Food Stylist Bridget Sargeson
Indexer Hilary Bird

**Hummingbird Bakery corporate
branding and company graphic
design** Sue Thedens
Illustrations Debbie Adamson

First published in 2010
by Ryland Peters & Small
20–21 Jockey's Fields
London WC1R 4BW

519 Broadway, 5th Floor
New York, NY 10012

www.rylandpeters.com

The recipes in this book have
been published previously by
Ryland Peters & Small in
The Hummingbird Bakery Cookbook

10 9 8

Text © Tarek Malouf and
The Hummingbird Bakery 2009, 2010
Design and photographs
© Ryland Peters & Small 2009, 2010

Printed in China

ISBN: 978 1 84975 075 2

Notes

• All spoon measurements are level,
unless otherwise specified.

• All eggs are medium, unless otherwise
specified. It is generally recommended
that free-range eggs be used. Uncooked
or partially cooked eggs should not be
served to the very young, the very old,
those with compromised immune
systems, or to pregnant women.

• Ovens should be preheated to the
specified temperature. Recipes in this
book were tested using a regular oven.
If using a fan-assisted oven, follow the
manufacturer's instructions for adjusting
temperatures.

For digital editions visit
rylandpeters.com/apps.php

contents

Welcome to The Hummingbird Bakery

I first thought about opening The Hummingbird Bakery after spending Thanksgiving with cousins in North Carolina. I wondered why there wasn't a place in London that made American-style cakes to a high standard. On subsequent trips to the USA, and New York in particular, I visited various bakeries that made all the goodies that I enjoyed eating, especially cupcakes. At that point, cupcakes seemed to be unknown in London – at least, they were hard to buy.

I started planning the Bakery in 2002. A unit in Portobello Road in London's Notting Hill came up by chance and I immediately jumped on it. It proved to be heaven-sent because as soon as the shop opened, a lot of high-profile customers began to write and speak about it. On Saturdays, when the famous market is on, tourists flock to Portobello and they were soon queueing up to try our cupcakes.

It will probably come as no surprise that we sell far more cupcakes than anything else. They seem to be popular because of their cute size, the childhood memories they evoke and their sheer versatility. Our best-selling cupcakes are vanilla with pink frosting, which reflects our female-dominated customer base, and red velvet, simply because they look and taste so distinctive. Muffins are also extremely popular – they were always favourites in school lunchboxes when I was at school – and they are great for any occasion because you can make them savoury or sweet.

I'm so pleased to share my favourite recipes for cupcakes and muffins with you in this little book. I hope you enjoy baking them as much we all do at The Hummingbird Bakery. Do take a look at our baking tips on the following page before you start.

Tarek Malouf

baking tips

Most of our recipes have been collected from old friends and relatives, so they come from a variety of sources and use many different cooking methods. We have modified them so they should turn out exactly as they do in our shops. Here are some of our baking tips to ensure that you get the best results from the recipes in this book.

• It sounds simple, but please do follow the recipes exactly as written! Baking is a chemical reaction, so any experimentation with the recipe amounts can potentially cause a recipe to fail.

• Some of our baking methods may seem unconventional to experienced bakers, but the recipes will work if followed exactly.

• Don't rush when measuring out ingredients and following the cooking method. In haste, we can all forget to measure out or add a certain ingredient!

• Make sure that your bicarbonate of soda/baking soda and baking powder have not passed their expiry date.

• Don't substitute self-raising flour for plain/all-purpose flour – this will affect the recipe!

• When making muffins, paper cases can be filled as much as three-quarters full but may overflow a little and create a 'muffin top'! This is normal.

• When making cupcakes, only ever fill the paper cases two-thirds full.

• When creaming butter and sugar together, always make sure you do this until the mixture is light and fluffy, usually at least a good 5 minutes.

• After adding flour to a mixture, don't overbeat as this will overwork the flour and make the cake dense. Simply beat or stir until just incorporated.

• Get an oven thermometer that you can hook into your oven permanently. This ensures that your oven temperature is accurate and well calibrated.

• Ovens vary greatly, so use our suggested cooking times as a rough guide. First bake to the shorter cooking time, and then check every few minutes until finished.

• Please don't open your oven until at least the minimum recommended time has passed. Too much cold air coming in from an open oven door can cause cakes to sink or not rise properly. Also, the more items baking in the oven at the same time, the longer the baking time might be.

• Cupcakes and muffins are only ready when a skewer inserted in the middle comes out clean. They are not automatically ready when the recommended time is up!

frostings

These frostings make enough to frost
12 cupcakes. Dye the Vanilla or Cream
Cheese frostings any shade you like
with a couple of drops of food colouring
mixed in until evenly incorporated.
At the Hummingbird, we like our
cupcake frostings in pretty candy colours,
but you can choose any colour you like.

vanilla

250 g/2 cups icing/confectioners' sugar, sifted

80 g/5 tablespoons unsalted butter, at room temperature

2 tablespoons whole milk

a couple of drops of pure vanilla extract

Beat the icing/confectioners' sugar and butter in a freestanding electric mixer with a paddle attachment (or use a handheld electric whisk) on medium-slow speed until the mixture comes together and is well mixed. Turn the mixer down to slow speed.

Combine the milk and vanilla extract in a separate bowl, then add to the butter mixture a little at a time. Once all the milk has been incorporated, turn the mixer up to high speed. Beat until the frosting is light and fluffy, at least 5 minutes. The longer the frosting is beaten, the fluffier and lighter it becomes.

cream cheese

300 g/2⅓ cups icing/confectioners' sugar, sifted

50 g/3 tablespoons unsalted butter, at room temperature

125 g/4 oz. cream cheese, cold

Beat the icing/confectioners' sugar and butter in a freestanding electric mixer with a paddle attachment (or use a handheld electric whisk) on medium-slow speed until the mixture comes together and is well mixed.

Add the cream cheese in one go and beat until it is completely incorporated. Turn the mixer up to medium-high speed. Beat until the frosting is light and fluffy, at least 5 minutes. Do not overbeat, as it can quickly become runny.

ginger

100 ml/⅓ cup whole milk

1 large piece of fresh ginger, peeled and chopped into 4 chunks

400 g/3¼ cups icing/confectioners' sugar, sifted

125 g/1 stick unsalted butter, at room temperature

grated zest of ½ unwaxed lemon

Put the milk and ginger pieces in a bowl, cover and refrigerate for a few hours.

Beat the icing/ confectioners' sugar, butter and lemon zest in a freestanding electric mixer with a paddle attachment (or use a handheld electric whisk) on medium-slow speed until the mixture comes together and is well mixed. Turn the mixer down to slow speed. Strain the ginger-infused milk and slowly pour into the butter mixture. Once incorporated, turn the mixer up to high speed. Beat until the frosting is light and fluffy, at least 5 minutes.

chocolate

300 g/2⅓ cups icing/confectioners' sugar, sifted

100 g/6½ tablespoooons unsalted butter, at room temperature

40 g/⅓ cup unsweetened cocoa powder, sifted

3 tablespoons whole milk

Beat the icing/confectioners' sugar, butter and cocoa in a freestanding electric mixer with a paddle attachment (or use a handheld electric whisk) on medium-slow speed until the mixture comes together and is well mixed.

Turn the mixer down to slow speed. Add the milk to the butter mixture a little at a time. Once all the milk has been incorporated, turn the mixer up to high speed. Beat until the frosting is light and fluffy, about 5 minutes. The longer the frosting is beaten, the fluffier and lighter it becomes.

lavender

2 tablespoons whole milk

1 tablespoon dried lavender flowers

250 g/2 cups icing/confectioners' sugar, sifted

80 g/5 tablespoons unsalted butter, at room temperature

a couple of drops of purple food colouring (optional)

Put the milk and dried lavender flowers in a bowl, cover and refrigerate for a few hours.

Beat the icing/confectioners' sugar, butter and purple food colouring, if using, in a freestanding electric mixer with a paddle attachment (or use a handheld electric whisk) on medium-slow speed until the mixture comes together and is well mixed. Turn the mixer down to slow speed. Strain the lavender-infused milk and slowly pour into the butter mixture. Once incorporated, turn the mixer up to high speed. Beat until the frosting is light and fluffy, at least 5 minutes.

green tea

250 g/2 cups icing/confectioners' sugar, sifted

80 g/5 tablespoons unsalted butter, at room temperature

2½ tablespoooons Matcha green tea powder

2 tablespoons whole milk

Beat the icing/confectioners' sugar, butter and Matcha powder in a freestanding electric mixer with a paddle attachment (or use a handheld electric whisk) on medium-slow speed until the mixture comes together and is well mixed.

Turn the mixer down to a slower speed. Slowly pour in the milk, then when it is all incorporated, turn the mixer up to high speed. Beat until the frosting is light and fluffy, at least 5 minutes.

cupcakes

vanilla cupcakes

120 g/1 cup plain/all-purpose flour

140 g/scant ¾ cup caster sugar

1½ teaspoons baking powder

a pinch of salt

40 g/3 tablespoons unsalted butter,
at room temperature

120 ml/½ cup whole milk

1 egg

¼ teaspoon pure vanilla extract

1 quantity Vanilla Frosting (page 11)

food colouring of your choice (optional)

hundreds and thousands/nonpareils or
other edible sprinkles, to decorate

*a 12-cup cupcake pan,
lined with paper cases*

Makes 12

Preheat the oven to 170°C (325°F) Gas 3.

Put the flour, sugar, baking powder, salt and butter in a freestanding electric mixer with a paddle attachment (or use a handheld electric whisk) and beat on slow speed until you get a sandy consistency and everything is combined. Gradually pour in half the milk and beat until the milk is just incorporated.

Whisk the egg, vanilla extract and remaining milk together in a separate bowl, then pour into the flour mixture and continue beating until just incorporated (scrape any unmixed ingredients from the side of the bowl with a spatula). Continue mixing for a couple more minutes until the mixture is smooth. Do not overmix.

Spoon the mixture into the paper cases until two-thirds full and bake in the preheated oven for 20–25 minutes, or until light golden and the cake bounces back when touched. A skewer inserted in the centre should come out clean. Leave the cupcakes to cool slightly in the pan before turning out onto a wire rack to cool completely.

Tint the Vanilla Frosting with food colouring, if using. When the cupcakes are cold, spoon the Vanilla Frosting on top and decorate with hundreds and thousands/nonpareils.

red velvet cupcakes

60 g/4 tablespoons unsalted butter,
at room temperature

150 g/¾ cup caster sugar

1 egg

1 tablespoon unsweetened cocoa
powder

2 tablespoons red food colouring
(we use Dr. Oetker Red Food Colouring)

½ teaspoon pure vanilla extract

120 ml/½ cup buttermilk

150 g/1 cup plus 2 tablespoons plain/
all-purpose flour

½ teaspoon bicarbonate of soda/
baking soda

1½ teaspoons white vinegar

1 quantity Cream Cheese Frosting
(page 11)

*a 12-cup cupcake pan,
lined with paper cases*

Makes 12

Preheat the oven to 170°C (325°F) Gas 3.

Put the butter and the sugar in a freestanding electric mixer with a
paddle attachment (or use a handheld electric whisk) and beat on
medium speed until light and fluffy. Turn the mixer up to high speed,
slowly add the egg and beat until everything is well incorporated.

In a separate bowl, mix together the cocoa, red food colouring and
vanilla extract to make a thick, dark paste. Add to the butter mixture
and mix thoroughly until evenly combined and coloured (scrape any
unmixed ingredients from the side of the bowl with a rubber spatula).
Turn the mixer down to slow speed and slowly pour in half the
buttermilk. Beat until well mixed, then add half the flour and beat
until everything is well incorporated. Repeat this process until all the
buttermilk and flour have been added. Scrape down the side of the
bowl again. Turn the mixer up to high speed and beat until you have
a smooth, even mixture. Turn the mixer down to low speed and add
the bicarbonate of soda/baking soda and vinegar. Turn up the speed
again and beat for a couple more minutes.

Spoon the mixture into the paper cases until two-thirds full and bake
in the preheated oven for 20–25 minutes, or until the cake bounces
back when touched. A skewer inserted in the centre should come
out clean. Leave the cupcakes to cool slightly in the pan before
turning out onto a wire rack to cool completely. To make red crumbs
for sprinkling on top of the frosted cupcakes, slice a thin sliver off
the top of a couple of the baked cakes and crumble between your
fingertips. When the cupcakes are cold, spoon the Cream Cheese
Frosting on top and dust with the red crumbs.

chocolate cupcakes

100 g/¾ cup plus 2 tablespoons plain/all-purpose flour

2½ tablespoons unsweetened cocoa powder

140 g/a scant ¾ cup caster sugar

1½ teaspoons baking powder

a pinch of salt

40 g/3 tablespoons unsalted butter, at room temperature

120 ml/½ cup whole milk

1 egg

¼ teaspoon pure vanilla extract

1 quantity Chocolate Frosting (page 13), or Vanilla or Cream Cheese Frosting (page 11)

chocolate vermicelli or edible silver balls/dragees, to decorate

a 12-cup cupcake pan, lined with paper cases

Makes 12

Preheat the oven to 170°C (325°F) Gas 3.

Put the flour, cocoa, sugar, baking powder, salt and butter in a freestanding electric mixer with a paddle attachment (or use a handheld electric whisk) and beat on slow speed until you get a sandy consistency and everything is combined.

Whisk the milk, egg and vanilla extract together in a bowl, then slowly pour about half into the flour mixture, beat to combine and turn the mixer up to high speed to get rid of any lumps.

Turn the mixer down to a slower speed and slowly pour in the remaining milk mixture (scrape any unmixed ingredients from the side of the bowl with a rubber spatula). Continue mixing for a couple more minutes until the mixture is smooth. Do not overmix.

Spoon the mixture into the paper cases until two-thirds full and bake in the preheated oven for 20–25 minutes, or until the cake bounces back when touched. A skewer inserted in the centre should come out clean. Leave the cupcakes to cool slightly in the pan before turning out onto a wire rack to cool completely.

When the cupcakes are cold, spoon the Chocolate, Vanilla or Cream Cheese Frosting on top and decorate with chocolate vermicelli or silver balls/dragees.

lemon cupcakes

120 g/1 cup plain/all-purpose flour

150 g/¾ cup caster sugar

1½ teaspoons baking powder

2 tablespoons grated lemon zest,
plus extra to decorate

40 g/3 tablespoons unsalted butter,
at room temperature

120 ml/½ cup whole milk

1 egg

lemon frosting

250 g/2 cups icing/confectioners' sugar,
sifted

80 g/5 tablespoons unsalted butter,
at room temperature

2 tablespoons grated lemon zest

a couple of drops of yellow food
colouring (optional)

2 tablespoons whole milk

*a 12-cup cupcake pan,
lined with paper cases*

Makes 12

Preheat the oven to 170°C (325°F) Gas 3.

Put the flour, sugar, baking powder, lemon zest and butter in a freestanding electric mixer with a paddle attachment (or use a handheld electric whisk) and beat on slow speed until you get a sandy consistency and everything is combined. Gradually pour in the milk and beat until just incorporated.

Add the egg to the flour mixture and continue beating until just incorporated (scrape any unmixed ingredients from the side of the bowl with a rubber spatula). Continue mixing for a couple more minutes until the mixture is smooth. Do not overmix.

Spoon the mixture into the paper cases until two-thirds full and bake in the preheated oven for 20–25 minutes, or until the cake bounces back when touched. A skewer inserted in the centre should come out clean. Leave the cupcakes to cool slightly in the pan before turning out onto a wire rack to cool completely.

For the lemon frosting: Beat together the icing/confectioners' sugar, butter, lemon zest and yellow food colouring, if using, in a freestanding electric mixer with a paddle attachment (or use a handheld electric whisk) on medium-slow speed until the mixture comes together and is well mixed. Turn the mixer down to a slower speed. Slowly pour in the milk, then when it is all incorporated, turn the mixer up to high speed. Beat until the frosting is light and fluffy, at least 5 minutes.

When the cupcakes are cold, spoon the lemon frosting on top and decorate with a little lemon zest.

strawberry cheesecake cupcakes

120 g/1 cup plain/all-purpose flour

140 g/a scant ¾ cup caster sugar

1½ teaspoons baking powder

a pinch of salt

40 g/3 tablespoons unsalted butter, at room temperature

120 ml/½ cup whole milk

½ teaspoon pure vanilla extract

1 egg

12 large strawberries, chopped into small pieces

200 g/6½ oz. digestive biscuits/ graham crackers

1 quantity Cream Cheese Frosting (page 11)

a 12-cup cupcake pan, lined with paper cases

Makes 12

Preheat the oven to 170°C (325°F) Gas 3.

Put the flour, sugar, baking powder, salt and butter in a freestanding electric mixer with a paddle attachment (or use a handheld electric whisk) and beat on slow speed until you get a sandy consistency and everything is combined.

Pour in the milk and vanilla extract and beat on medium speed until all the ingredients are well mixed (scrape any unmixed ingredients from the side of the bowl with a rubber spatula). Add the egg and beat well for a few minutes.

Divide the chopped strawberries between the paper cases. Spoon the cupcake mixture on top until two-thirds full and bake in the preheated oven for 20–25 minutes, or until light golden and the cake bounces back when touched. A skewer inserted in the centre should come out clean. Leave the cupcakes to cool slightly in the pan before turning out onto a wire rack to cool completely.

Roughly break up the digestive biscuits/graham crackers and put them in a food processor. Process until finely ground. When the cupcakes are cold, spoon the Cream Cheese Frosting on top and finish with a sprinkling of finely ground biscuits.

black bottom cupcakes

1 quantity Cream Cheese Frosting
(page 11) (optional)

chocolate base

190 g/1½ cups plain/all-purpose flour

120 g/½ cup plus 1 tablespoon caster
sugar

½ teaspoon bicarbonate of soda/
baking soda

40 g/½ cup unsweetened cocoa powder,
plus extra to decorate

40 ml/¼ cup sunflower oil

1½ teaspoons white vinegar

½ teaspoon pure vanilla extract

cheesecake filling

140 g/4½ oz. cream cheese

60 g/⅓ cup caster sugar

1 egg

½ teaspoon pure vanilla extract

a pinch of salt

100 g/⅔ cup chocolate chips

a 12-cup cupcake pan,
lined with paper cases

Makes 12

Preheat the oven to 170°C (325°F) Gas 3.

For the chocolate base: Put the flour, sugar, bicarbonate of soda/
baking soda and cocoa in a large bowl and mix with a handheld
electric whisk on slow speed until well mixed.

Put the oil, vinegar, vanilla extract and 125 ml/½ cup water in a bowl
and whisk to combine. While the electric whisk is running in the
flour bowl, slowly add the liquid ingredients, increasing the speed
of the blender as the mixture thickens. Continue to beat until all the
ingredients are incorporated (scrape any unmixed ingredients from
the side of the bowl with a rubber spatula). Spoon the mixture into
the paper cases until two-thirds full and set aside.

For the cheesecake filling: Beat the cream cheese, sugar, egg,
vanilla extract and salt in a freestanding electric mixer with a paddle
attachment (or use a handheld electric whisk) on medium speed
until smooth and fluffy. Stir in the chocolate chips by hand but don't
overmix otherwise the cream cheese will start to split.

Scoop about 1 tablespoon of the cheesecake filling on top of the
cupcake mixture in the cases and bake in the preheated oven for
about 20 minutes, or until the cupcakes are firm to the touch and
they have an even golden colour on the cheesecake filling. Don't
overcook as the cheesecake will become very dry and crumbly.
Leave the cupcakes to cool slightly in the pan before turning out
onto a wire rack to cool completely.

When the cupcakes are cold, spoon the Cream Cheese Frosting on
top, if using, and decorate with a light sprinkling of cocoa.

lavender cupcakes

120 ml/½ cup whole milk

3 tablespoons dried lavender flowers

120 g/1 cup plain/all-purpose flour

140 g/a scant ¾ cup caster sugar

1½ teaspoons baking powder

40 g/3 tablespoons unsalted butter,
at room temperature

1 egg

1 quantity Lavender Frosting (page 13)

12 small sprigs of lavender (optional)

*a 12-cup cupcake pan,
lined with paper cases*

Makes 12

Put the milk and dried lavender flowers in a bowl, cover and refrigerate for a few hours.

Preheat the oven to 170°C (325°F) Gas 3.

Put the flour, sugar, baking powder and butter in a freestanding electric mixer with a paddle attachment (or use a handheld electric whisk) and beat on slow speed until you get a sandy consistency and everything is combined.

Strain the lavender-infused milk and slowly pour into the flour mixture, beating well until all the ingredients are well mixed. Add the egg and beat well (scrape any unmixed ingredients from the side of the bowl with a rubber spatula).

Spoon the mixture into the paper cases until two-thirds full and bake in the preheated oven for 20–25 minutes, or until the cake bounces back when touched. A skewer inserted in the centre should come out clean. Leave the cupcakes to cool slightly in the pan before turning out onto a wire rack to cool completely.

When the cupcakes are cold, spoon the Lavender Frosting on top and decorate with a sprig of lavender, if using.

hazelnut and chocolate cupcakes

100 g/¾ cup plus 1 tablespoon plain/all-purpose flour

2½ tablespoons unsweetened cocoa powder

140 g/a scant ¾ cup caster sugar

1½ teaspoons baking powder

a pinch of salt

40 g/3 tablespoons unsalted butter, at room temperature

120 ml/½ cup whole milk

1 egg

120 g/½ cup hazelnut and chocolate spread (such as Nutella)

about 36 whole, shelled hazelnuts, to decorate

hazelnut and chocolate frosting

250 g/2 cups icing/confectioners' sugar, sifted

80 g/5 tablespoons unsalted butter, at room temperature

2 tablespoons whole milk

80 g/⅓ cup hazelnut and chocolate spread (such as Nutella)

*a 12-cup cupcake pan,
lined with paper cases*

Makes 12

Preheat the oven to 170°C (325°F) Gas 3.

Put the flour, cocoa, sugar, baking powder, salt and butter in a freestanding electric mixer with a paddle attachment (or use a handheld electric whisk) and beat on slow speed until you get a sandy consistency and everything is combined.

Slowly pour the milk into the flour mixture, beating well until all the ingredients are well mixed. Add the egg and beat well (scrape any unmixed ingredients from the side of the bowl with a rubber spatula).

Spoon the mixture into the paper cases until two-thirds full and bake in the preheated oven for about 20 minutes, or until the cake bounces back when touched. Leave the cupcakes to cool slightly in the pan before turning out onto a wire rack to cool completely.

When the cupcakes are cold, hollow out a small hole in the centre of each one and fill with hazelnut and chocolate spread before frosting.

For the hazelnut and chocolate frosting: Beat the icing/confectioners' sugar and butter in a freestanding electric mixer with a paddle attachment (or use a handheld electric whisk) on medium-slow speed until the mixture comes together and is well mixed. Turn the mixer down to a slower speed. Slowly pour in the milk, then when it is all incorporated, turn the mixer up to high speed. Beat until the frosting is light and fluffy, at least 5 minutes.

Stir in the hazelnut and chocolate spread by hand until evenly mixed into the frosting. When the cupcakes are cold, spoon the frosting on top and finish with about 3 hazelnuts per cupcake.

banana and chocolate cupcakes

120 g/1 cup plain/all-purpose flour

140 g/a scant ¾ cup caster sugar

1 tablespoon baking powder

1 teaspoon ground cinnamon

1 teaspoon ground ginger

a pinch of salt

80 g/5 tablespoons unsalted butter, at room temperature

120 ml/½ cup whole milk

2 eggs

1 ripe banana, peeled and mashed

1 quantity Chocolate Frosting (page 13)

40 g/1½ oz. chocolate, grated with a cheese grater into shavings

*a 12-cup cupcake pan,
lined with paper cases*

Makes 12

Preheat the oven to 170°C (325°F) Gas 3.

Put the flour, sugar, baking powder, cinnamon, ginger, salt and butter in a freestanding electric mixer with a paddle attachment (or use a handheld electric whisk) and beat on slow speed until you get a sandy consistency and everything is combined.

Slowly pour the milk into the flour mixture, beating well until all the ingredients are well mixed. Add the eggs and beat well (scrape any unmixed ingredients from the side of the bowl with a rubber spatula).

Stir in the mashed banana by hand until evenly dispersed.

Spoon the mixture into the paper cases until two-thirds full and bake in the preheated oven for 20 minutes, or until golden and the cake bounces back when touched. Leave the cupcakes to cool slightly in the pan before turning out onto a wire rack to cool completely.

When the cupcakes are cold, spoon the Chocolate Frosting on top and finish with the chocolate shavings.

green tea cupcakes

120 ml/½ cup whole milk

3 green tea bags

100 g/¾ cup plus 1 tablespoon plain/all-purpose flour

2 tablespoons unsweetened cocoa powder

140 g/a scant ¾ cup caster sugar

1½ teaspoons baking powder

a pinch of salt

40 g/3 tablespoons unsalted butter, at room temperature

1 egg

¼ teaspoon pure vanilla extract

1 quantity Green Tea Frosting (page 13)

Matcha green tea powder, to decorate

*a 12-cup cupcake pan,
lined with paper cases*

Makes 12

Put the milk and green tea bags in a bowl, cover and refrigerate for a few hours.

Preheat the oven to 170°C (325°F) Gas 3.

Put the flour, cocoa, sugar, baking powder, salt and butter in a freestanding electric mixer with a paddle attachment (or use a handheld electric whisk) and beat on slow speed until you get a sandy consistency and everything is combined.

Remove the green tea bags from the infused milk and combine with the egg and vanilla extract. Slowly pour half into the flour mixture, beating well until all the ingredients are well mixed. Turn the mixer up to high speed and beat well to make sure there are no lumps. Turn the speed back down to medium-slow and slowly pour in the remaining milk mixture (scrape any unmixed ingredients from the side of the bowl with a rubber spatula). Continue mixing for a couple more minutes until the mixture is smooth.

Spoon the mixture into the paper cases until two-thirds full and bake in the preheated oven for 20–25 minutes, or until the cake bounces back when touched. A skewer inserted in the centre should come out clean. Leave the cupcakes to cool slightly in the pan before turning out onto a wire rack to cool completely.

When the cupcakes are cold, spoon the Green Tea Frosting on top and decorate with a light sprinkling of Matcha powder.

peaches and cream cupcakes

120 g/1 cup plain/all-purpose flour

140 g/a scant ¾ cup caster sugar

1½ teaspoons baking powder

a pinch of salt

40 g/2 tablespoons unsalted butter, at room temperature

120 ml/½ cup whole milk

1 egg

¼ teaspoon pure vanilla extract

400 g/14 oz. canned peaches, sliced

1 quantity Vanilla Frosting (page 11)

soft light brown sugar, to decorate (optional)

a 12-cup cupcake pan, lined with paper cases

Makes 12

Preheat the oven to 170°C (325°F) Gas 3.

Put the flour, sugar, baking powder, salt and butter in a freestanding electric mixer with a paddle attachment (or use a handheld electric whisk) and beat on slow speed until you get a sandy consistency and everything is combined. Gradually pour in half the milk and beat until the milk is just incorporated.

Whisk the egg, vanilla extract and remaining milk together in a separate bowl for a few seconds, then pour into the flour mixture and continue beating until just incorporated (scrape any unmixed ingredients from the side of the bowl with a rubber spatula). Continue mixing for a couple more minutes until the mixture is smooth. Do not overmix.

Divide the sliced peaches between the paper cases so that the base of each case is covered. Spoon the cupcake mixture on top until two-thirds full and bake in the preheated oven for 20–25 minutes, or until light golden and the cake bounces back when touched. A skewer inserted in the centre should come out clean. Leave the cupcakes to cool slightly in the pan before turning out onto a wire cooling rack to cool completely.

When the cupcakes are cold, spoon the Vanilla Frosting on top and finish with a light sprinkling of soft light brown sugar, if using.

pumpkin cupcakes

120 g/1 cup plain/all-purpose flour

140 g/a scant ¾ cup caster sugar

1 tablespoon baking powder

1½ teaspoons ground cinnamon,
plus extra to decorate

a pinch of salt

40 g/3 tablespoons unsalted butter,
at room temperature

120 ml/½ cup whole milk

2 eggs

200 g/6½ oz. canned pumpkin purée

1 quantity Cream Cheese Frosting
(page 11)

*a 12-cup cupcake pan,
lined with paper cases*

Makes 12

Preheat the oven to 170°C (325°F) Gas 3.

Put the flour, sugar, baking powder, cinnamon, salt and butter in
a freestanding electric mixer with a paddle attachment (or use a
handheld electric whisk) and beat on slow speed until you get
a sandy consistency and everything is combined. Gradually pour
in the milk and beat until well mixed.

Add the eggs to the mix and beat well (scrape any unmixed
ingredients from the side of the bowl with a rubber spatula). Stir in
the pumpkin purée by hand until evenly dispersed.

Spoon the mixture into the paper cases until two-thirds full and bake
in the preheated oven for 20 minutes, or until golden and the cake
bounces back when touched. Leave the cupcakes to cool slightly
in the pan before turning out onto a wire rack to cool completely.

When the cupcakes are cold, spoon the Cream Cheese Frosting on
top and finish with a light sprinkling of cinnamon.

coconut and pineapple cupcakes

120 g/1 cup plain/all-purpose flour

140 g/a scant ¾ cup caster sugar

1½ teaspoons baking powder

a pinch of salt

40 g/3 tablespoons unsalted butter, at room temperature

120 ml/½ cup coconut milk

½ teaspoon pure vanilla extract

1 egg

9 canned pineapple rings, chopped into small pieces

desiccated coconut, to decorate

coconut frosting

250 g/2 cups icing/confectioners' sugar, sifted

80 g/5 tablespoons unsalted butter, at room temperature

2 tablespoons coconut milk

a 12-cup cupcake pan, lined with paper cases

Makes 12

Preheat the oven to 170°C (325°F) Gas 3.

Put the flour, sugar, baking powder, salt and butter in a freestanding electric mixer with a paddle attachment (or use a handheld electric whisk) and beat on slow speed until you get a sandy consistency and everything is combined.

Mix the coconut milk and vanilla extract in a separate bowl, then beat into the flour mixture on medium speed until well combined. Add the egg and beat well (scrape any unmixed ingredients from the side of the bowl with a rubber spatula).

Divide the chopped pineapple between the paper cases. Spoon the cupcake mixture on top until two-thirds full and bake in the preheated oven for 20–25 minutes, or until light golden and the cake bounces back when touched. A skewer inserted in the centre should come out clean. Leave the cupcakes to cool slightly in the pan before turning out onto a wire rack to cool completely.

For the coconut frosting: Beat the icing/confectioners' sugar and butter together in a freestanding electric mixer with a paddle attachment (or use a handheld electric whisk) on medium-slow speed until the mixture comes together and is well mixed. Turn the mixer down to a slower speed and slowly pour in the coconut milk. Once all the milk has been incorporated, turn the mixer up to high speed. Continue beating until the frosting is very white, light and fluffy, 5–10 minutes.

When the cupcakes are cold, spoon the coconut frosting on top and finish with a sprinkling of desiccated coconut.

marshmallow cupcakes

120 g/1 cup plain/all-purpose flour

140 g/a scant ¾ cup caster sugar

1½ teaspoons baking powder

a pinch of salt

45 g/3 tablespoons unsalted butter, at room temperature

120 ml/½ cup whole milk

1 egg

¼ teaspoon pure vanilla extract

12 medium pink marshmallows

200 g/6½ oz. mini marshmallows, for the frosting

1 quantity Vanilla Frosting (page 11)

edible glitter, to decorate

a 12-cup cupcake pan, lined with paper cases

Makes 12

Preheat the oven to 170°C (325°F) Gas 3.

Put the flour, sugar, baking powder, salt and butter in a freestanding electric mixer with a paddle attachment (or use a handheld electric whisk) and beat on slow speed until you get a sandy consistency and everything is combined. Gradually pour in half the milk and beat until the milk is just incorporated.

Whisk the egg, vanilla extract and remaining milk together in a separate bowl for a few seconds, then pour into the flour mixture and continue beating until just incorporated (scrape any unmixed ingredients from the side of the bowl with a rubber spatula). Continue mixing for a couple more minutes until the mixture is smooth. Do not overmix.

Spoon the mixture into the paper cases until two-thirds full and bake in the preheated oven for 20–25 minutes, or until light golden and the cake bounces back when touched. A skewer inserted in the centre should come out clean. Leave the cupcakes to cool slightly in the pan before turning out onto a wire rack to cool completely.

Put the medium marshmallows in a heatproof bowl over a pan of simmering water. Leave until melted and smooth. When the cupcakes are cold, hollow out a small section in the centre of each one and fill with a dollop of melted marshmallow. Leave to cool.

Stir the mini marshmallows into the Vanilla Frosting by hand until evenly dispersed. Spoon the frosting on top of the cupcakes and decorate with edible glitter.

ginger cupcakes

120 g/1 cup plain/all-purpose flour

140 g/a scant ¾ cup caster sugar

1½ teaspoons baking powder

½ teaspoon ground cinnamon

¼ teaspoon ground allspice

a pinch of salt

40 g/3 tablespoons unsalted butter, at room temperature

120 ml/½ cup whole milk

1 egg

¼ teaspoon pure vanilla extract

200 g/6½ oz. stem ginger in syrup, finely chopped (and syrup reserved), plus extra to decorate

1 quantity Ginger Frosting (page 11)

a little grated lemon zest, to decorate

a 12-cup cupcake pan, lined with paper cases

Makes 12

Preheat the oven to 170°C (325°F) Gas 3.

Put the flour, sugar, baking powder, cinnamon, allspice, salt and butter in a freestanding electric mixer with a paddle attachment (or use a handheld electric whisk) and beat on slow speed until you get a sandy consistency and everything is combined. Gradually pour in half the milk and beat until just incorporated. Whisk the egg, vanilla extract and remaining milk together in a separate bowl for a few seconds, then pour into the flour mixture and continue beating until just incorporated (scrape any unmixed ingredients from the side of the bowl with a rubber spatula). Continue mixing for a couple more minutes until the mixture is smooth. Stir in the chopped ginger by hand until evenly dispersed.

Spoon the mixture into the paper cases until two-thirds full and bake in the preheated oven for 20–25 minutes, or until golden brown and the cake bounces back when touched. Meanwhile, pour 100 ml/ ⅓ cup of the reserved ginger syrup and 100 ml/⅓ cup water into a small saucepan and bring to the boil. Boil until reduced by one-third. When the hot cupcakes come out of the oven, pour a small amount of syrup over each one. Leave the cupcakes to cool slightly in the pan before turning out onto a wire rack to cool completely.

When the cupcakes are cold, spoon the Ginger Frosting on top and finish with chopped stem ginger and lemon zest.

muffins

carrot and zucchini muffins

2 eggs

200 g/1 cup soft/packed light brown sugar

80 ml/⅓ cup sunflower oil

260 g/2 cups plain/all-purpose flour

2 teaspoons baking powder

2 teaspoons ground cinnamon

80 ml/⅓ cup natural/plain yogurt

½ teaspoon pure vanilla extract

120 g/a scant cup chopped walnuts

3 carrots, grated

1 zucchini/courgette, grated

a 12-cup muffin pan, lined with paper cases

Makes 12

Preheat the oven to 170°C (325°F) Gas 3.

Put the eggs, sugar and oil in an electric mixer with a paddle attachment (or use a handheld electric whisk) and beat on slow speed until well combined. In a separate bowl, sift together the flour, baking powder and cinnamon, then add to the egg mixture. Beat until everything is well incorporated.

Add the yogurt and vanilla extract and mix through until well combined. Stir in the walnuts, carrots and zucchini/courgette with a wooden spoon until evenly dispersed.

Spoon the mixture into the paper cases until two-thirds full and bake in the preheated oven for 25–30 minutes, or until deep golden and the muffin bounces back when touched. A skewer inserted in the centre should come out clean. Leave the muffins to cool slightly in the pan before turning out onto a wire rack to cool completely.

ham and mushroom muffins

50 g/3½ tablespoons butter
½ small onion, finely chopped
80 g/1 cup button mushrooms, chopped
360 g/2¾ cups plain/all-purpose flour
2½ teaspoons baking powder
250 g/2 cups grated cheddar cheese
220 ml/1 cup whole milk
1 egg
80 g/2½ oz. smoked ham, finely chopped
sea salt and freshly ground black pepper

a 12-cup muffin pan,
lined with paper cases

Makes 12

Preheat the oven to 170°C (325°F) Gas 3.

Melt the butter in a saucepan over medium heat, then fry the onion and mushrooms until cooked. Season with sea salt and black pepper. Set aside.

Put the flour, baking powder and cheese in a large bowl. In a separate bowl, mix the milk and egg together, then slowly pour into the flour mixture and beat with a handheld electric whisk until all the ingredients are well mixed.

Stir in the onion, mushrooms and chopped ham with a wooden spoon until evenly dispersed.

Spoon the mixture into the paper cases until two-thirds full and bake in the preheated oven for 30–35 minutes, or until deep golden and the muffin bounces back when touched. A skewer inserted in the centre should come out clean. Leave the muffins to cool slightly in the pan before turning out onto a wire rack to cool completely.

spinach and cheese muffins

30 g/2 tablespoons butter

½ small red onion, finely chopped

360 g/2¾ cups plain/all-purpose flour

2½ teaspoons baking powder

1 teaspoon cayenne pepper

250 g/2 cups grated cheddar cheese

220 ml/1 cup whole milk

1 egg

130 g/4 oz. baby spinach leaves

*a 12-cup muffin pan,
lined with paper cases*

Makes 12–14

Preheat the oven to 170°C (325°F) Gas 3.

Melt the butter in a saucepan over medium heat, then fry the onion until cooked. Set aside.

Put the flour, baking powder, cayenne and cheese in a large bowl. In a separate bowl, mix the milk and egg together, then slowly pour into the flour mixture and beat with a handheld electric whisk until all the ingredients are well mixed. Stir in the onion and spinach with a wooden spoon until evenly dispersed.

Spoon the mixture into the paper cases until two-thirds full and bake in the preheated oven for 30–35 minutes, or until deep golden and the muffin bounces back when touched. A skewer inserted in the centre should come out clean. Leave the muffins to cool slightly in the pan before turning out onto a wire rack to cool completely.

chocolate muffins

2 eggs

200 g/1 cup caster sugar

130 g/1 cup plain/all-purpose flour

50 g/6 tablespoons unsweetened cocoa powder

2 teaspoons baking powder

a pinch of salt

160 ml/⅔ cup whole milk

¼ teaspoon pure vanilla extract

160 g/1 stick plus 3 tablespoons unsalted butter, melted

120 g/4 oz. dark/bittersweet chocolate, roughly chopped

a 12-cup muffin pan,
lined with paper cases

Makes 12

Preheat the oven to 170°C (325°F) Gas 3.

Put the eggs and sugar in a freestanding electric mixer with a paddle attachment (or use a handheld electric whisk) and beat until pale and well combined.

In a separate bowl, sift together the flour, cocoa, baking powder and salt. In another bowl, combine the milk and vanilla extract. Gradually beat these 2 mixtures alternately into the egg mixture little by little (scrape any unmixed ingredients from the side of the bowl with a rubber spatula). Beat until all the ingredients are well incorporated.

Stir in the melted butter with a wooden spoon until well incorporated, then stir in the chocolate until evenly dispersed.

Spoon the mixture into the paper cases until two-thirds full and bake in the preheated oven for about 30 minutes, or until the muffin bounces back when touched. A skewer inserted in the centre should come out clean. Leave the muffins to cool slightly in the pan before turning out onto a wire rack to cool completely.

blueberry muffins

360 g/2¾ cups plain/all-purpose flour

370 g/1¾ cups caster sugar

1 teaspoon salt

1½ teaspoons baking powder

½ teaspoon bicarbonate of soda/
baking soda

375 ml/1½ cups buttermilk

1 egg

½ teaspoon pure vanilla extract

70 g/5 tablespoons unsalted butter,
melted

250 g/1 pint blueberries

*a 12-cup muffin pan,
lined with paper cases*

Makes 12–14

Preheat the oven to 170°C (325°F) Gas 3.

Put the flour, sugar, salt, baking powder and bicarbonate of soda/
baking soda in a freestanding electric mixer with a paddle
attachment (or use a handheld electric whisk) and beat on slow
speed until combined.

Put the buttermilk, egg and vanilla extract into a bowl and mix to
combine. Slowly pour into the flour mixture and beat until all the
ingredients are incorporated.

Pour in the melted butter and beat until the butter has just been
incorporated, then turn the mixer up to medium speed and beat
until the dough is even and smooth.

Finally, gently fold in the blueberries with a wooden spoon until
evenly dispersed.

Spoon the mixture into the paper cases until two-thirds full and bake
in the preheated oven for 20–25 minutes, or until golden brown and
the muffin bounces back when touched. A skewer inserted in the
centre should come out clean. Leave the muffins to cool in the pan
before turning out onto a wire rack to cool completely.

banana and cinnamon muffins

350 g/2⅔ cups plain/all-purpose flour

¾ teaspoon salt

1½ teaspoons baking powder

½ teaspoon bicarbonate of soda/
baking soda

2 teaspoons ground cinnamon,
plus extra to sprinkle

160 g/¾ cup caster sugar, plus extra
to sprinkle

375 ml/1½ cups buttermilk

1 egg

½ teaspoon pure vanilla extract

70 g/5 tablespoons unsalted butter,
melted

400 g/1¾ cups mashed banana

*a 12-cup muffin pan,
lined with paper cases*

Makes 14–16

Preheat the oven to 170°C (325°F) Gas 3.

Put the flour, sugar, salt, baking powder, bicarbonate of soda/baking soda and cinnamon in a large bowl and beat with a handheld electric whisk until combined.

Put the buttermilk, egg and vanilla extract in a bowl and mix to combine. Slowly pour into the flour mixture and beat on slow speed until all the ingredients are incorporated.

Pour in the melted butter and beat until incorporated. Stir in the bananas with a wooden spoon until evenly dispersed.

Spoon the mixture into the paper cases until two-thirds full and sprinkle a little extra sugar and cinnamon over the tops. Bake in the preheated oven for 20–30 minutes, or until golden brown and the muffin bounces back when touched. A skewer inserted in the centre should come out clean. Leave the muffins to cool slightly in the pan before turning out onto a wire rack to cool completely.

maple and pecan muffins

350 g/2⅔ cups plain/all-purpose flour

160 g/¾ cup caster sugar

¾ teaspoon salt

1½ teaspoons baking powder

½ teaspoon bicarbonate of soda/
baking soda

375 ml/1½ cups buttermilk

1 egg

½ teaspoon pure vanilla extract

70 g/5 tablespoons unsalted butter,
melted

240 g/1⅔ cups shelled pecans, chopped,
plus 12 pecan halves to decorate

200 ml/¾ cup pure maple syrup

*a 12-cup muffin pan,
lined with paper cases*

Makes 14–16

Preheat the oven to 170°C (325°F) Gas 3.

Put the flour, sugar, salt, baking powder and bicarbonate of soda/
baking soda in a large bowl and beat with a handheld electric whisk
until combined.

Put the buttermilk, egg and vanilla extract in a bowl and mix to
combine. Slowly pour into the flour mixture and beat on slow speed
until all the ingredients are incorporated.

Pour in the melted butter and beat until incorporated. Stir in half the
maple syrup and all the pecans with a wooden spoon.

Spoon the mixture into the paper cases until two-thirds full and
drizzle the remaining maple syrup over the tops. Finish with a pecan
half in the centre of each one. Bake in the preheated oven for about
20–30 minutes, or until golden brown and the muffin bounces back
when touched. A skewer inserted in the centre should come out
clean. Leave the muffins to cool slightly in the pan before turning
out onto a wire rack to cool completely.

websites and mail order

UK

Cakes Cookies & Crafts Shop
www.cakescookiesandcraftsshop.co.uk
Tel: +44 (0)1524 389 684

Online suppliers of every kind of baking equipment: lots of paper cupcake cases, pans, silicone moulds, cookie cutters, edible decorations and more.

Jane Asher
www.janeasher.com
Tel: +44 (0)20 7584 6177

Cake and sugarcraft supplier for all your decorating needs.

John Lewis
www.johnlewis.com
Tel: +44 (0)8456 049 049

A lovely range of bakeware, from vintage-style mixing bowls and measuring cups to ceramic cupcake cups and heart-shaped and silicone cupcake pans.

Lakeland
www.lakeland.co.uk
Tel: +44 (0)1539 488 100

Huge selection of kitchen and baking equipment, such as cupcake pans, cake decorations, storage containers, etc., as well as a stand designed especially to display cupcakes.

Steamer Trading
www.mycookshop.com
Tel: +44 (0)1273 403000

Family-owned chain of cook shops throughout the UK, with an online store.

US

Confectionery House
www.confectioneryhouse.com
Tel: +1 518 279 4250

Stockists of paper cases in every colour and size, for every occasion, as well as sprinkles and edible decorations

Cool Cupcakes
www.coolcupcakes.com
Tel: +1 800 797 2887

Baking enthusiasts and the cupcake-obsessed will find sanding sugar, edible glitter and sprinkles in a rainbow of colours, plus paper cases and three-, four-, five- and six-tier cupcake stands on this comprehensive website.

Crate & Barrel
www.crateandbarrel.com
Tel: +1 800 967 6696

Store and online supplier of kitchenware, such as muffin pans, silicone bakeware, seasonal paper cases and useful cupcake carriers.

Sur La Table
www.surlatable.com
Tel: +1 800 243 0852

Cupcake and muffin pans, tiered cake stands and more.

Williams-Sonoma
www.williams-sonoma.com
Tel: +1 877 812 6235

Cupcake and muffin pans, cake stands and more.

Wilton
www.wilton.com

The site to browse for all manner of baking and decorating supplies. Packed with patterned and themed paper cases, sprinkles, food colouring and decorations to suit every possible occasion and theme.

index